How to Start an Online Business

For

Under $20

By

Russell Lee

This book is for personal use only. Do not duplicate or reproduce this content.

Copyright © 2016

LeeWritingServices.com - All Rights Reserved

Disclaimer

By reading this book, the reader understands and acknowledges that:

1) The content in this book only contains opinions that are based on the author's own experiences. The reader is always advised to use their own best judgment in determining which business ideas will work for them.

2) The author is not responsible for how the information in this book affects the reader's finances.

3) There are no guarantees being made by the author about how much money the reader will make if any at all.

Introduction to Online Businesses

If you are reading this book, then you are most likely interested in starting an online business for yourself. One of the biggest benefits of starting an online business is the low amount of expense involved in running it. When you look at a traditional brick-and-mortar business, a business owner has to worry about paying their lease, utilities, employee wages, inventory and commercial taxes. Online businesses cut out most of these expenses, which you will learn more about while reading this book.

So, why start a business at all? In the current world we live in today, more people are going to have to go into business for themselves if they ever want to make any decent money. The days of depending on a traditional

9-to-5 job are over. You simply cannot live off of the wages that employers pay you these days. If you are lucky enough to have a decent paying job, then you still won't have the security of knowing it will be there in five or ten years because employers famously lay off people more often these days. Companies simply look for any excuse to save a buck, even if it means cutting the jobs of hard working people that have devoted their lives to the company. Therefore, you need to create your own opportunity and this book will help guide you. Since most of you probably don't have a lot of money to start a big business with, this book will show you how to start a business while investing less than $20.

Types of Online Businesses

There are many types of online businesses that you can start up, but you shouldn't just jump into anything. There are a lot of so-called "gurus" on the internet that sell advice to people on how to make quick money online. The truth is that running an online business is hard work, so don't expect it to be a walk in the park. The only difference between online businesses and traditional businesses are the fact that you don't have to worry about paying for the expense of running a physical location.

Services

The online business you choose should be something that is interesting to you or something you are at least good at doing. This is the other problem with gurus that try to push you into a particular business. Their recommendation for a business may not be something that you would like to do. Therefore, you will likely fail at it because you won't be motivated enough to see it through. Instead, what you need to do in order to choose a business is to sit down and make a list of everything you are good at doing. After you make that list, think about ways you can turn these skills into a money making business on the internet. For example, if you are good at drawing pictures and making illustrations, then you can sell this skill as a service online. You don't even have to worry about setting up your own website because there are plenty of popular online marketplaces that let you advertise your services for free. A really good website to sell services on is www.Fiverr.com. They allow you to sell any small service for $5. Eventually, after you establish your account then you can include additional options that people can select to get more work done. These options are called "gig extras" and they give the seller a chance to earn additional money. To see an example visit: http://www.fiverr.com/russflex

Wholesale Products

Most retail businesses revolve around buying wholesale products from their manufacturer or another dealer that sells items in bulk quantity. The benefit of buying items in bulk amounts is that you get them for a huge discount. When you turn around and sell them individually, then you will make a big profit in the end. This is the most common business model, whether you run a business offline or online.

Original Products

Original products are something that you can create yourself and then sell on a website or online auction. Now this business option is not for everybody because you have to be skilled enough to be able to design your own products. For people that have a lot of money, you could always hire Chinese workers overseas to manufacture your products for you. Of course, this is not an option if you are looking to spend under $20 to start your online business. If that is the case then you need to pick a product that can be made cheaply and with cheap materials. For example, if you are an artist then you could paint pictures and then sell them on eBay. They actually have a category on eBay for artists selling their own work. All you need are basic materials for your painting, like paper, board, paint, brush and so on. You could go to an arts & crafts store to pick up these materials cheaply. To stay under $20 on your startup, you can just create an illustration on paper and then sell it for $10. Once you get the $10, use that money to invest in more drawing materials to produce more paintings or illustrations. As the orders come in you can keep purchasing more and so on.

    Now if you are interested in an actual product that resembles something you would find in a retail store, then you need spend more money on materials. Either that or try to find a venture capitalist to invest in your product. Venture capitalists are basically investors that help finance startup businesses. What you need to do is prepare a business plan that describes your product and how you intend to sell it. The same applies if you go to a bank to get a traditional loan. The loan officer will want to see how you plan on making money so that they can trust you enough to pay back the loan.

A Business Plan

A business plan is something that everyone must write if they plan on creating a successful business. You can be sure that offline startup companies write business plans because it is the only way they'll be able to convince a venture capitalist or loan officer at a bank to give them startup funds. These people want to see a layout of the business, such as the mission statements, income statements, and financial statements. Basically, you would have to convince these people that your business is going to make money. A business plan outlines exactly how the money will be made and in what timeframe.

People tend to get lazier with online businesses. For one thing, they are very cheap to start up (if you didn't guess that already). This makes people pay less attention to the formalities of starting their business because it doesn't cost them much money. However, a business plan is still crucial to write no matter how much money you need for your business. Even if you aren't writing it to get money from someone else, you can still use it as a guide while running your business. You'll need to plan out how you will get your business online, how you will market it and how much you want to make within the first year. If you don't plan any of these things and just throw a website together, that is not a real business. Unfortunately, this is what most people do and their online businesses fail quickly. You need to treat the online business like you would if you were opening up a shop in your local town. Don't let the virtual part of the business fool you into thinking it isn't the same thing because it is.

If you need help writing your business plan, you can go to Google and search for templates. You can even hire a freelance writer to help you write the business plan. Check out LeeWritingServices.com to get assistance with that.

Typical Expenses

When you connect your business through other websites, like Fiverr or eBay, you are only doing it in order to utilize their traffic and gain customers. That is the only reason why you would ever want to pay 10-20% commissions out to another company. But, if you want to open a true online business that is totally unique and not run off another company's website, then you will have to be prepared to spend money. Fortunately, you won't have to spend a lot of money because online startup costs are cheap.

Let's break down every expense that you will have in getting your online business started.

Domain Name

These are the addresses that people type into their browser in order to find a particular website. For online businesses, you will want to register a domain name that relates to the niche of your business. Either that or it can be the name of your actual business. The registration of a domain name is around $10 PER YEAR. That's not bad at all.

Web Hosting

This is what you will need in order to hold the files that make up your website. There are plenty of web hosting companies on the internet, which offer all different kinds of hosting options. The type of hosting you choose normally depends on how sophisticated your website files are, especially if they are PHP scripts or JavaScript. But for starters, you should just put up a basic website that is not complicated and simple for you to host. This means you will be able to purchase shared hosting. This is the cheapest hosting you can purchase.

There are free hosting websites, like 000webhost.com, that allows you to host files for free. Of course, you will have bandwidth and storage limits, but this is fine because you won't have a lot of traffic in the beginning. If you want to pay for shared hosting then you can get unlimited bandwidth and storage. Sharing hosting rates are only around $4.84 per month. If you purchase by the year, then you can be entitled to an even bigger discount. But, only upgrade to paid hosting when you start getting more traffic and feel the need for it. Otherwise, stick with free hosting in the beginning.

Marketing

When it comes to advertising and marketing, getting customers to an online business is actually harder than a brick-and-mortar business. At least with a physical location you can attract people that are passing by in their cars or simply cater to your local area of people that don't have computers. With an online business, you have to get your website name and URL in front of people's faces. That is no easy task for a startup online business that has to compete with millions of other websites in the search engines.

    The marketing and advertising of an online business are something many people overlook. They just assume their website will start getting traffic once it is uploaded and actively ready on the internet. This is not going to happen because people on the internet need to know your site exists. It just won't magically appear in the Google search engine or in people's inbox. You have to get your website address out there so that it will be discovered and eventually recognized by many people. There are various methods in order to market your online business, both paid and free methods. Until you get more experience on the internet, you should start with free methods of advertising. The reason being is that paid advertising can cost you a lot of money and provide little results if you don't know what you're doing. It will be better to try with free advertising and establish your website a little bit before you go towards the bigger route of paid advertising.

Free Marketing on Craigslist

You are probably wondering, "Can free advertising actually get people to my website?" The answer is absolutely! There are ways to utilize the traffic of other popular websites by advertising your business on them. For example, Craigslist is a free classified ads website where people can post up ads on almost anything. Craigslist actually gives you two methods of free advertising. They have their simple classified ads section where you can post up your business advertisement. This should only contain your pitch along with some basic contact information, such as your phone number. If you put your website, you have to make sure it is based locally to the city you post under or else the post will get flagged. However, there is a way around this if you just have a generic website that isn't based in one location. There is a FORUM section on Craigslist that often gets overlooked by online marketers. In this forum section, you can post up a comment featuring your advertisement and link, and it will be seen by everyone on that board. You won't get flagged for it either. The best part is that the forum is not just seen by locals. The Craigslist forum allows you to post up your message to **EVERY** local area forum under the same topic. This is something you cannot do with the classified ad method.

Yahoo Answers

Another website you can use for free advertising is Yahoo, especially the Yahoo Answers section. This is where you can answer questions that other people post up. The idea is for you to find a question that will give you an excuse to answer it with a link to your online business.

For example, someone may ask a question like "Where can I find cheap diamond rings?" If you happen to run an online jewelry store then this is the perfect opportunity for you to answer that question with a link to your online business. This also creates a backlink that will allow other people who see the question to click on it and visit your website. This backlink will also improve your website's ranking in the Google search engine.

TALLY UP THE TOTAL

So, let's add up all of the startup costs for your online business.

Domain Name: **$10** (per year)

Hosting: **Free**

Marketing: **Free**

TOTAL START UP EXPENSE:
$10

As you can see, to get your online business started on the internet will cost you only $10. Think about how much less that is in comparison to a traditional brick-and-mortar business. Now you are probably saying to yourself, "What about inventory?" Well, those costs depend on the type of business you are running and if you already have an existing physical business. For example, if you already run a store in your local town, then you already have the inventory available to sell your products online. Therefore, you won't have to incur any additional expenses when you bring your existing business to the internet.

If you don't have any existing businesses and you want to sell products, then you will likely have to get some kind of inventory. If you have no money saved and no way to get a loan to buy inventory, then you may need to think of a new business that you can do online that won't require you to buy inventory. As previously mentioned, you could start a business selling services that you can deliver through the internet. This could be writing, graphic design, website design and so on. Then once you make enough money from selling services, you can use that money to purchase inventory for a product selling business. You just have to think creative, which may mean starting a business that you don't want to do in order to finance a business that you do want to do.

Don't Give Up!

This is probably the best piece of advice that you can get when starting any business, particularly an online business. Because the upfront investment is so minimal with an online business, it is very easy for somebody to quit if they aren't getting customers fast enough. They will likely tell themselves that it is a waste of time or that nobody is looking at their website. It is easy to get paranoid when running an online business because you don't physically see your customers. The only way you can tell if anybody is visiting your website is to install a tracking system, like Google Analytics. This web software will be able to tell you the number of hits you receive each day and where they came from. This is a free service that Google offers, so you should certainly take advantage of it.

Like any business, it could take you a few years to get it off the ground and running. Don't quit your day job until you are seeing a consistent return of money coming in from your online business. Then you can devote more time to expanding the business by implementing more marketing techniques or whatever else you can think of. The important thing you have to realize is that all successful businesses took a lot of hard work and patience to get to where they are now. The only way you are going to have patience with your own business is if you believe in the product or service you are selling. If you are just trying to make a million dollars within a month, then you are going to set yourself up for a disappointment. Remember to stick with your business plan and set a realistic goal for the amount of money you want to make within a year. Then keep expanding upon that as you get more customers.

GOOD LUCK!

www.ingramcontent.com/pod-product-compliance
Lightning Source LLC
Chambersburg PA
CBHW070735180526
45167CB00004B/1759